Television Reporters

BY DAVE CUPP AND CECILIA MINDEN

The Child's World

Published by The Child's World®
1980 Lookout Drive • Mankato, MN 56003-1705
800-599-READ • www.childsworld.com

Acknowledgments
The Child's World®: Mary Berendes, Publishing Director
The Design Lab: Design
Jody Jensen Shaffer: Editing
Pamela J. Mitsakos: Photo Research

Photos
Alexander Podshivalov/123RF.com: 5; AlexRaths/
iStock.com: 10-11; angelhell/iStock.com: mic; antb/
Shutterstock.com: 14; Boogich/iStock.com: 6-7; cjp/
iStock.com: 8; claudiaveja/iStock.com: cover, 1, 12;
Dave Cupp: 20-21; Gunold Brunbauer/Dreamstime.
com: 22; JBryson/iStock.com: 4; Jim Carpenter: 9;
Judy Beyer: 16; krestafer/iStock.com: 13; Pavel L Photo
and Video/Shutterstock.com: 18; Photodisc: camera;
Stockbyte: notepad; Sveta/iStock.com: 17

ISBN 9781626870192
LCCN 2013947295

Printed in the United States of America
Mankato, MN
December, 2013
PA02191

ABOUT THE AUTHORS

Dave Cupp was the News Director and Anchor for WVIR for twenty-five years. He is now an Assistant Professor in the School of Journalism and Mass Communication at the University of North Carolina.

Dr. Cecilia Minden is a university professor and reading specialist with classroom and administrative experience in grades K–12. She earned her PhD in reading education from the University of Virginia.

CONTENTS

Hello, My Name Is Annika.

Hello. My name is Annika. Many people live and work in my neighborhood. Each of them helps the neighborhood in different ways.

I thought of all the things I like to do. I like to search the computer and find interesting facts. I like to share what I've learned with my friends. I like talking to people. How could I help my neighborhood when I grow up?

Do you like being on camera?

I Could Be a TV Reporter!

Television (TV) reporters are good at reading and writing. They search for information and interesting facts. They help people in the neighborhood share their stories. Best of all, they get to be on TV!

When Did This Job Start?
TV news reports began in the early 1940s. They were once a day and lasted fifteen minutes. These reports became longer and more detailed in the mid-1950s. Videotape allowed reporters to cover more stories. Today, Americans rely on TV reporters for news.

Learn About This Neighborhood Helper!

The best way to learn is to ask questions. Words such as *who*, *what*, *where*, *when*, and *why* will help me learn about being a TV reporter.

Where Can I Learn More?
The National Association of Broadcasters
1771 N Street NW
Washington, DC 20036

Radio-Television News Directors Association
1600 K Street NW, Suite 700
Washington, DC 20006

Asking a TV reporter questions will help you learn more about the job.

Who Can Become a TV Reporter?

Girls and boys who are good at writing, speaking, and listening might want to become TV reporters. A good TV reporter also needs to know how to ask questions. A TV reporter is not shy!

TV reporters are important helpers in the neighborhood. They help people find out what is going on around them.

How Can I Explore This Job?

Does your community have a local TV station? Call and ask if you can visit. You might even get a tour of the newsroom! Ask any reporters you meet what they like best about their job.

TV reporters help people learn about important events.

Meet a TV Reporter!

This is Dana Hackett. Dana is a TV reporter at station WVIR-TV/DT in Charlottesville, Virginia. When she is not reporting the news, she likes to dance, play her flute, travel, and root for her favorite sports teams.

Dana reports the news in Charlottesville.

Where Can I Learn to Be a TV Reporter?

Most TV reporters go to college. Dana went to the University of North Carolina. She learned to gather facts and write well. She also took classes in history, science, and math. A TV reporter needs to know about many different things.

Most TV reporters take a variety of classes in college.

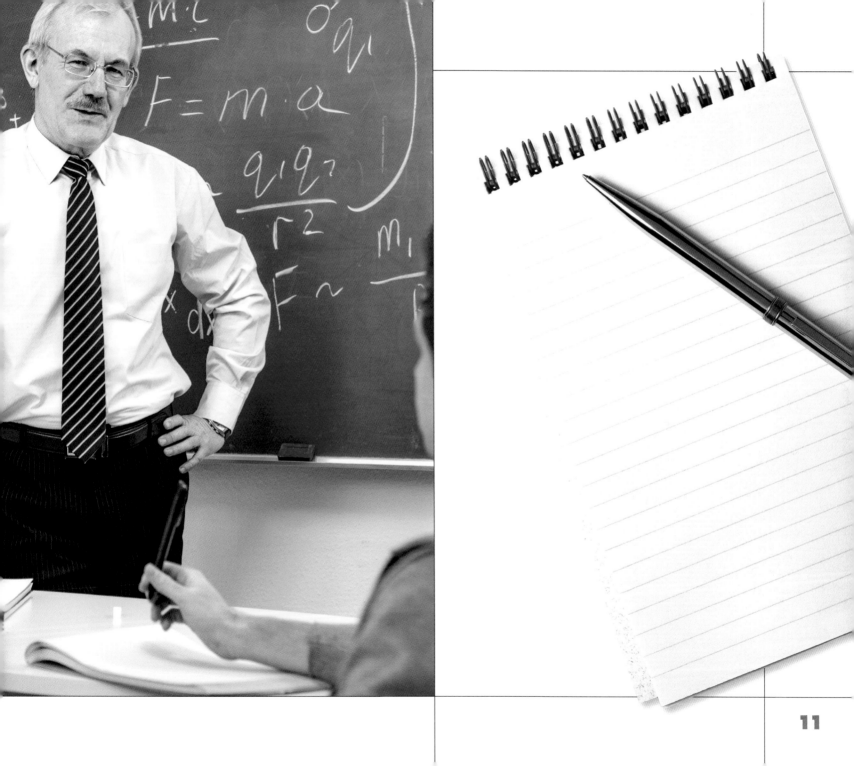

How Much School Will I Need?

TV reporters usually have a four-year college degree. Most study journalism in college.

TV reporters sometimes sit behind a desk to deliver the news.

What Does a TV Reporter Need to Do the Job?

Dana and her crew need video cameras to record events. This allows the people watching television to see what is happening in the story. Dana also needs a **microphone** so people can hear what she has to say.

Dana needs to talk to the audience when she shares the news. She does this by looking into a **teleprompter**. The teleprompter allows Dana to look at the audience and read the news at the same time!

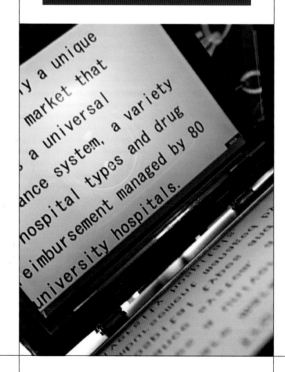

What Are Some Tools I Will Use?
- Laptop computer
- Microphone
- Satellite videophones
- Teleprompter
- Video camera and video editing equipment

Teleprompters have large letters so they are easy to read.

What Clothes Will I Wear?

For men:

- Suit and tie

For women:

- Blazer and blouse
- Skirt or slacks

TV reporters need to be comfortable in front of a camera.

Where Does a TV Reporter Work?

Dana's day usually starts with a meeting in the newsroom in Charlottesville. This is where stories are assigned. She spends time in an office making phone calls or checking facts on the computer. Then Dana goes into Charlottesville's different neighborhoods to interview people. Finally, she comes back to the newsroom to write her story. TV reporters have to be quick because the stories are often due at the end of the day!

What's It Like Where I'll Work?

A newsroom is often a large room. Most people in the newsroom work quickly. They need to finish their stories on time. They use computers and often spend a lot of time on the telephone. TV reporters might work any time of day or night. They need to cover stories as they are happening. TV reporters often travel. They sometimes even have to work in dangerous situations.

Dana's job takes her to many different places in Charlottesville. One day she may write a story about a fire. Another day she may write a story about a local election. What an exciting job!

TV reporters often have to make phone calls and do research on the computer to prepare for a story.

Who Works with TV Reporters?

Many people work at WVIR-TV with Dana. They all come together every day to make sure the news gets to people in Charlottesville. Many people work behind the camera. One important person behind the camera is the producer. The producer runs the whole show.

What other Jobs Might I Like?
- Camera operator
- Meteorologist
- News director
- Newspaper reporter
- Radio reporter
- Sports announcer
- Videographer

Producers play an important role at TV stations.

Reporters from around the world cover everything from sports to entertainment. This reporter is in Moscow.

When Does a TV Reporter Get to Travel?

Sometimes TV reporters get to travel to other countries. TV reporters from around the world cover big events such as the Olympics. Each TV reporter at a major event may come from a different country and speak a different language. They are all working quickly to create **accurate** news stories!

How Might My Job Change?
TV reporters often start at a small, local TV station. They usually work as a researcher or production assistant. Some work as reporters behind the scenes. TV reporters eventually gain more experience and go on to report more stories in front of a camera. They sometimes leave smaller stations to take jobs at larger ones.

I Want to Be a TV Reporter!

I think being a TV reporter would be a great way to be a neighborhood helper. Someday you may see me on the evening news!

Is This Job Growing?
The need for TV reporters will grow more slowly than other jobs.

Why Don't You Try Being a TV Reporter?

Do you think you would like to be a TV reporter? Read this list of facts.

- First pig builds home.
- Wolf comes along and blows it down.
- Second pig builds home.
- Wolf comes along and blows it down.
- Third pig builds home.
- Wolf cannot blow down the house.

Maybe one day you'll be reporting the news!

- Wolf tries to get in through chimney.
- Pig tricks wolf.
- House and pig are saved.

Talk to your friends to see if they know anything about what happened. Do you have enough facts to write a news story? What pictures could you draw to help tell the story? Now write the story. Then read the story to your friends just like a real TV reporter would read to an audience.

Good TV reporters know how to gather information and share it in an interesting way.

GLOSSARY

accurate (AK-yur-ut) completely correct

microphone (MY-kruh-fohn) an instrument that uses electric currents to make sound louder

teleprompter (TEL-uh-promp-tur) a special camera that people can read off of while reporting the news or giving a speech

LEARN MORE ABOUT TELEVISION REPORTERS

BOOKS

Byrum, R. T. *Television*. San Diego: Lucent Books, 2005.

Davis, Gary. *Working at a TV Station*. Danbury, CT: Children's Press, 1999.

Hayward, Linda. *A Day in the Life of a TV Reporter*. New York: Dorling Kindersley, 2001.

WEB SITES

Visit our home page for lots of links about television reporters:

www.childsworld.com/links

Note to Parents, Teachers, and Librarians: We routinely check our Web links to make sure they're safe, active sites—so encourage your readers to check them out!

INDEX